W9-CMT-844

LAKES, RIVERS, AND STREAMS

MINA FLORES

PowerKiDS
press

NEW YORK

Published in 2017 by The Rosen Publishing Group, Inc.
29 East 21st Street, New York, NY 10010

Editor: Theresa Morlock
Book Design: Michael Flynn
Interior Layout: Tanya Dellaccio

Photo Credits: Cover Jaros/Shutterstock.com; p. 5 Photography by Byron Tanaphol Prukston/Getty Images; p. 6 Leemage/Getty Images; p. 7 Kazakova Maryia/Shutterstock.com; p. 9 Bucchi Francesco/Shutterstock.com; p. 10 ronnybas/Shutterstock.com; p. 11 Josef Hanus/Shutterstock.com; p. 12 https://commons.wikimedia.org/wiki/File:RedRiverMeandersArkansas1.jpg; p. 13 John Coletti/Getty Images; p. 14 Sarah Martinet/Getty Images; p. 15 https://commons.wikimedia.org/wiki/File:Uureg_Nuur.jpg; p. 17 Jan Cobb Photography Ltd/Getty Images; p. 18 Science & Society Picture Library/Getty Images; p. 19 Tupungato/Shutterstock.com; p. 21 Santiago Urquijo/Getty Images; p. 22 majeczka/Shutterstock.com.

Cataloging-In-Publication Data

Names: Flores, Mina.
Title: Lakes, rivers, and streams / Mina Flores.
Description: New York : PowerKids Press, 2017. | Series: Spotlight on earth science | Includes index.
Identifiers: ISBN 9781499425222 (pbk.) | ISBN 9781499425253 (library bound) | ISBN 9781499425239 (6 pack)
Subjects: LCSH: Rivers--Juvenile literature. | Lakes--Juvenile literature. | Stream ecology--Juvenile literature.
Classification: LCC GB1203.8 F56 2017 | DDC 577.63--d23

Manufactured in China

CPSIA Compliance Information: Batch #BW17PK For further information contact Rosen Publishing, New York, New York at 1-800-237-9932.

CONTENTS

EARTH'S FRESHWATER 4

THE WATER CYCLE 6

FLOWING WATER 8

STREAMS AND RIVERS 10

LAKES 12

WATERSHEDS 14

HOW WATER SHAPES THE WORLD 16

MAN-MADE WATERWAYS 18

HUMAN INTERVENTION 20

WHAT CAN WE DO? 22

GLOSSARY 23

INDEX 24

PRIMARY SOURCE LIST 24

WEBSITES 24

CHAPTER ONE

EARTH'S FRESHWATER

Freshwater **habitats** are vital to the survival of over 100,000 species, including people. However, less than three percent of all the water on Earth is freshwater! Freshwater is water that holds less than 0.5 parts per thousand of **dissolved** salts. Seawater, which takes up over 70 percent of Earth's surface, holds 35 parts per thousand of salts. Freshwater can be found in lakes, ponds, streams, rivers, and wetlands, as well as frozen in glaciers and stored as groundwater.

Lakes, rivers, and streams form habitats that support a variety of wildlife species. Without freshwater, people couldn't exist. We rely on it to drink, grow our food, and create electricity. Sadly, freshwater habitats are harmed by pollution and **climate change**. It's more important than ever to find ways to protect our freshwater habitats.

"Parts per thousand" is a unit used to explain how much of a solid substance is dissolved in a liquid. So, "35 parts per thousand" means that for every 1,000 grams of water, there are 35 grams of salt.

CHAPTER TWO

THE WATER CYCLE

Water goes through a cycle of evaporation, condensation, and precipitation. Evaporation is the process of water changing from liquid to vapor, or gas. When the sun heats a body of water, such as a lake, the heat causes the water's **molecules** to separate, changing its form from liquid to gas.

Condensation is the process of water vapor in the **atmosphere** changing to liquid. Clouds release water in the form of precipitation when it snows, rains, or hails. When water returns to the earth as rain, some of it ends up in lakes and rivers.

In 1580 a French scientist named Bernard Palissy published a work titled "Admirable Discourses" that helped provide the basis for our modern understanding of the water cycle. Unlike the scientists of his time who believed that oceans provided all the water to rivers, Palissy suggested that springs and rivers were fed by rainfall.

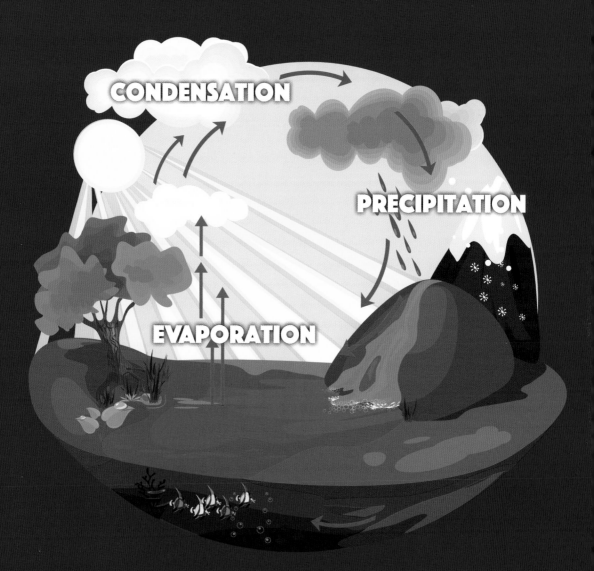

Gravity pulls precipitation to the ground, where it soaks into the soil or flows along the earth's surface. Water on the surface moves through watersheds, or areas of land in which water flows to the same place. All of the streams or rivers that flow to a pond, lake, bigger stream, river, or ocean are part of an area's watershed.

CHAPTER THREE

FLOWING WATER

Groundwater is freshwater below Earth's surface. A spring occurs when something causes this water to flow above the surface. There are five types of springs: gravity, artesian, seepage, tubular, and fissure.

Groundwater is stored in aquifers, or natural pockets in Earth's crust that hold water. In a gravity spring, an impermeable—or waterproof—layer in the earth prevents water from flowing downward. Instead, it flows to the side until it emerges as a spring, often flowing off a hill or cliff.

When water from an aquifer is pushed to the surface because of too much pressure in the surrounding layers of earth, it's an artesian spring. Seepage springs occur when groundwater is released into loose soil. Tubular springs are created when groundwater erodes, or wears away, rock and carves small tubes into it. In a fissure spring, groundwater spews out through cracks, or fissures, in the ground.

Some springs, such as Grand Prismatic Spring in Yellowstone National Park, are naturally hot. Hot springs occur when the temperature of the groundwater released in a spring is higher than the average temperature of the surrounding area.

CHAPTER FOUR

STREAMS AND RIVERS

The word "stream" applies to a natural **channel** of flowing water. A river is a stream of greater **volume**. Streams and rivers are shaped by water that makes its way down from higher **elevations** after precipitation. The rain filters into the ground or runs along the surface as runoff. Runoff is also caused by melting snow. Runoff forms streams and small rivers called tributaries, which join together to form larger rivers.

Rivers are often called Earth's veins. They carry the "blood" the planet needs to its "heart"—the ocean!

The measurement of water in a river is called streamflow. The streamflow of a river changes based on rainfall and runoff. When the streamflow of a river increases, it can wear away the surrounding land. Eroded pieces of land are carried downriver and deposited elsewhere, which is called deposition.

CHAPTER FIVE

LAKES

A lake is a large body of water that's surrounded by land. Water flows into a lake faster than it can evaporate or flow out. Lakes are formed in different ways. Some lakes, such as the Great Lakes in central North America, were shaped by the movement of glaciers. Oxbow lakes form when part of a river is blocked off from the rest. A man-made lake is called a reservoir.

This aerial photograph of the Red River in Arkansas shows several oxbow lakes that formed when the river changed course.

The Great Salt Lake in Utah is a saltwater lake. Saltwater lakes are sometimes called **terminal** lakes, because their water doesn't flow out to the ocean.

Most lakes contain freshwater from surface runoff or river flow. Some, however, contain salt water. Saltwater lakes such as the Dead Sea form when streams or runoff containing salts flow into a lake that doesn't have a river or stream flowing out of it. Instead, the water evaporates, leaving salt behind. These lakes are called saline lakes. Saline water can't be used to drink or water crops, and it's not as valuable to humans as freshwater.

13

CHAPTER SIX

WATERSHEDS

A watershed, also called a drainage basin, is an area of land that has a number of streams and rivers that all drain into the same place. Each watershed is made up of areas of high and low elevation. Because of gravity, water always travels from high to low. This is why water collects at a watershed's lowest point.

Watersheds are determined by the elevation levels that are present within them. Mountains may act as watershed boundaries because water will run down either one side or the other toward different watersheds.

A satellite view of Üüreg Nuur drainage basin in Mongolia.

Most watersheds drain into seas or oceans. When the bodies of water within an area don't have an ocean outlet, the watersheds are called endorheic. Endorheic watersheds usually form because natural barriers such as mountains and impermeable ground layers block the flow of water. Lakes in endorheic watersheds usually retain, or hold, more salt than those that empty into oceans. The Caspian Sea and the Great Salt Lake are two examples of large salt lakes in endorheic watersheds.

CHAPTER SEVEN

HOW WATER SHAPES THE WORLD

Water has the power to shape Earth's landscape. Processes of erosion, transportation, and deposition are being carried out by streams, rivers, and lakes all the time. Erosion occurs when water or wind wears down the earth into smaller pieces. Sediment—small pieces of eroded stone, sand, and soil—builds up in the water. Sediment is transported by water and deposited in another location. When river sediment builds up into a landmass at the mouth of a river, that new land is called a delta.

Wave movement on lakes can cause the shorelines to erode. The speed and power of waves is affected by the wind and rainfall over a lake. When rainfall is heavy, water levels rise, which allows lake water to reach farther inland. High winds increase the force of waves that crash against the shore. As they hit the shore, waves pull loose soil and rock into the lake, eroding the shoreline.

Ice can also change the landscape. This occurs when water enters cracks or ridges in rock. As the water freezes, it expands within the rock as solid ice, widening the crack and breaking the rock into pieces.

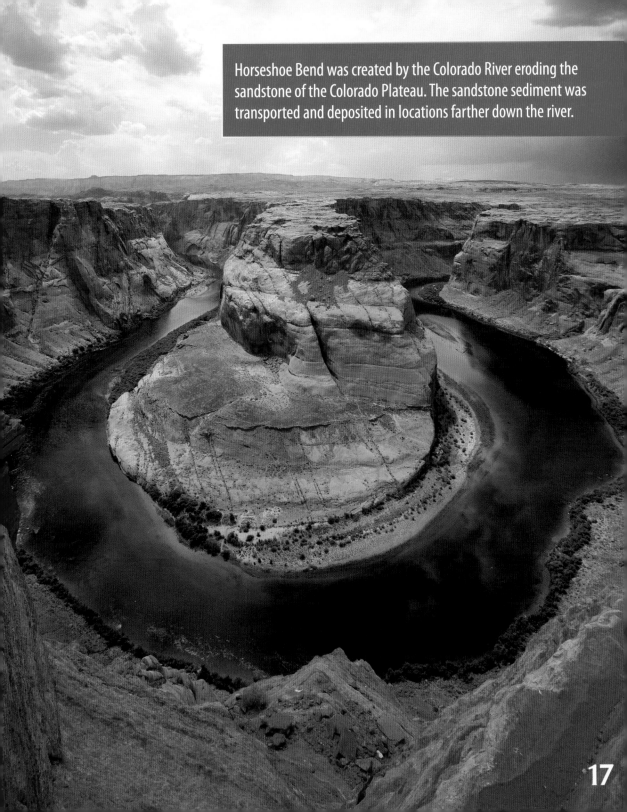

Horseshoe Bend was created by the Colorado River eroding the sandstone of the Colorado Plateau. The sandstone sediment was transported and deposited in locations farther down the river.

CHAPTER EIGHT

MAN-MADE WATERWAYS

People have created ways of guiding and controlling freshwater. A canal is a man-made waterway. Canals are used to ship goods and to direct water for irrigation. Irrigation is the process by which water is distributed to farmland to grow crops. Reservoirs are man-made lakes used to store water for a community's needs.

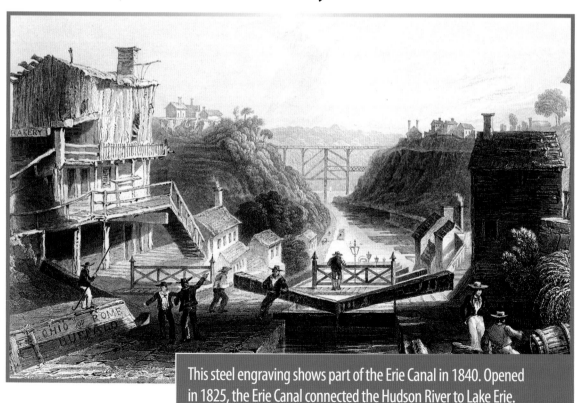

This steel engraving shows part of the Erie Canal in 1840. Opened in 1825, the Erie Canal connected the Hudson River to Lake Erie.

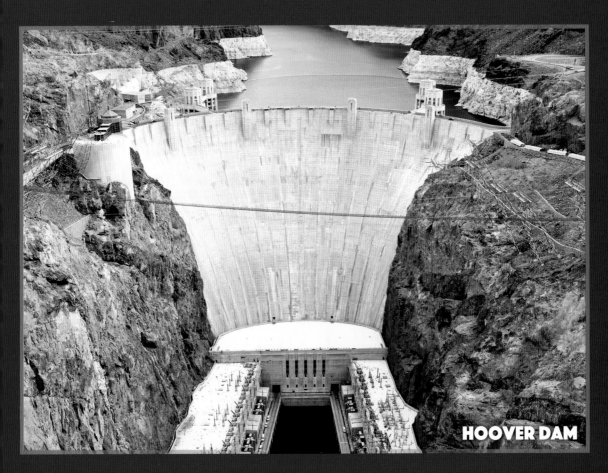

HOOVER DAM

Humans rely on water as a **resource** to create electricity. This is called hydroelectric power. Dams are built to hold water in a reservoir. As water is allowed through a dam and flows downward, it gains speed and energy. The pressure of the water is used to spin **turbines**. The spinning of these turbines generates, or produces, electricity.

While helpful to people, dams and canals disrupt freshwater habitats. This often has a bad result. For instance, some animals' migration routes are disrupted by new canals and reservoirs.

CHAPTER NINE

HUMAN INTERVENTION

We can't survive without freshwater. How has human **intervention** affected freshwater sources? Humans have been using water faster than it can be replaced naturally, which causes ponds and streams to dry up. Wetlands are intentionally drained to make more places for people to live.

Overuse also takes freshwater away from plants and animals that depend on it just as much as we do. The more water we use or redirect, the more limited freshwater habitats become. Overcrowding puts many freshwater creatures at risk of dying out.

Runoff from cities and farms pollutes water with chemicals. Large farms may use pesticides with harmful chemicals to kill insects that try to feed on crops. When these and other chemicals used in manufacturing wash into water, they can kill freshwater creatures or cause harmful changes that are passed on to their young.

River pollution is often caused by waste from industrial processes that discharge elements such as copper, zinc, and mercury into the water. Even if these elements don't kill wildlife at first, they are carried through the food chain, and can cause health problems

CHAPTER TEN

WHAT CAN WE DO?

Hydrologists are scientists who study water. They are working with civil engineers to come up with more **sustainable** ways for people to use freshwater. Using alternative energy resources such as wind and solar power helps relieve the pressure on our limited water supply. Changing the design of farm irrigation systems may play a key part in reducing the amount of water that is wasted by human activity.

You can protect lakes, rivers, and streams by thinking about how you use water in your daily life. Turn off the faucet while you brush your teeth, take shorter showers, and make sure that the washing machine and dishwasher are full before you do a load. We are all part of the problem, but we can all be part of the solution to the freshwater crisis.

GLOSSARY

atmosphere (AT-muh-sfeer) The mass of air that surrounds Earth.

channel (CHA-nuhl) A passage where water may run.

climate change (KLY-met CHANJ) Change in Earth's weather caused by human activity.

dissolve (dih-ZALHV) To mix into a liquid completely.

elevation (eh-luh-VAY-shun) Height above sea level.

habitat (HAA-buh-tat) The natural home for plants, animals, and other living things.

intervention (in-tuhr-VEN-shun) The act of taking action about something to affect the outcome.

molecule (MAH-luh-kyool) The smallest possible amount of something that has all the characteristics of that thing.

resource (RE-sors) A usable supply of something.

sustainable (sus-TAY-nuh-buhl) Able to last a long time.

terminal (TER-mih-null) Of, or relating to, the end of something.

turbine (TUR-byn) An engine with blades that are caused to spin by pressure from water, steam, or air.

volume (VAHL-yoom) The measurement of the amount of space that something takes up.

INDEX

A
aquifer, 8

C
canal, 18, 19
Caspian Sea, 15
climate change, 4
Colorado River, 17
condensation, 6, 7

D
dam, 19
Dead Sea, 12
delta, 16
deposition, 11, 16

E
Erie Canal, 18
erosion, 16
evaporation, 6, 7

G
Grand Prismatic Spring, 9
Great Lakes, 12
Great Salt Lake, 13, 15
groundwater, 8, 9

H
Hoover Dam, 19
Horseshoe Bend, 17
Hudson River, 19
hydroelectric power, 19
hydrologists, 22

L
Lake Erie, 18

O
oxbow lake, 12

P
Palissy, Bernard, 6
pollution, 20, 21
precipitation, 6, 7, 10

R
reservoir, 12, 18, 19
runoff, 10, 11, 12, 20

S
sediment, 16
springs, 6, 8, 9
streamflow, 11

T
tributaries, 10

U
Üüreg Nuur, 15

V
vapor, 6

W
water cycle, 6
watershed, 7, 14, 15

PRIMARY SOURCE LIST

Page 6
Portrait of Bernard Palissy. Chromolithograph. From *La Ciencia y sus Hombres* by Louis Figuier in Barcelona, Spain. Published 1881.

Page 12
Aerial photograph of Red River in Lafayette and Miller counties, Arkansas. May 27, 2011. Created from USDA/FSA Aerial Photography Field Office 2010 NAIP digital aerial orthophoto mosaic for Lafayette County, Arkansas.

Page 18
Lockport on the Erie Canal, New York, United States. Steel engraving. Created by William Tombleson.1840.

WEBSITES

Due to the changing nature of Internet links, PowerKids Press has developed an online list of websites related to the subject of this book. This site is updated regularly. Please use this link to access the list: www.powerkidslinks.com/soes/lakes